The Chairman of the Joint Chiefs of Staff, General Martin E. Dempsey, U.S. Army, has identified Mission Command as a critical enabler to the implementation of Joint Force 2020.[1] As such, a thorough examination of this leadership philosophy is warranted and necessary in order for the Chairman's vision to be realized. At its core, Mission Command consists of a clear commander's intent, delivered to subordinates through concise mission-type orders, in order to promote decentralized execution. Admittedly, even a casual observer of military history would note that these are not new concepts.[2] Its roots can be traced back to the leadership style of daring naval heroes like Admiral Horatio Lord Nelson and to the highly successful Prussian/German Army concept of *Auftragstaktik*.[3] The tenets of Mission Command are also firmly established in current joint and service doctrine like Joint Publication 3-0 "Joint Operations,"[4] Army Doctrine Publication 6-0 "Mission Command,"[5] and Marine Corps Doctrine Publication 1-0 "Marine Corps Operations."[6] However, in spite of all the historical and modern day references to Mission Command, it can be argued that there isn't a more widely acclaimed, battle proven leadership philosophy that is so infrequently and improperly applied.[7]

In his 2012 white paper, the Chairman correctly identifies micromanagement as one of the key challenges to Mission Command that, while always a potential impediment, becomes a significantly greater threat in this Information Age. He states, "In a network-enabled force, the commander can easily penetrate to the lowest level of the command and take over the fight."[8] Furthermore, the dramatic impact of the Internet and the 24-hour news cycle on public opinion also presents challenges. It has transformed the meaning of Strategic Corporal from a relatively positive term that denoted the transfer of increased capability and responsibility to lower levels, to a negative term that suggests mistakes made by the lowest ranking members of the military can lead to disastrous consequences at the operational and even strategic level.[9] The desire to prevent those types of mistakes can become powerful motivation for operational commanders to engage in micromanagement of their forces.[10]

In order to ensure that any potential challenges are overcome and that Mission Command is widely implemented and effective, three attributes have been correctly identified that the force must possess – intent, understanding, and trust.[11] Understandably, the leap has been made that these are leadership traits that individuals, including the commander, must possess as well.[12] However, a closer look at these attributes shows that while they accurately describe the traits of a relationship between a commander and his subordinates, they fail to accurately describe the traits of an individual. Instead, we must identify the individual leadership traits that will enable these relationship attributes. While there are undoubtedly many leadership traits that an operational commander must possess, two stand out as particularly important. Operational commanders must possess the leadership traits of boldness and interpersonal communication skills in order to effectively execute Mission Command in the face of technological advances that provide the motive and the means for micromanagement.

Before these leadership traits are examined, arguments from Network-Centric Warfare (NCW) proponents that discount the negative effects of information technology on Mission Command will be presented and ultimately addressed. Then a more in depth look at the philosophy of Mission Command based on operational theory and doctrine will occur, followed by a brief discussion of the definitions and characteristics of boldness and interpersonal communication skills. Next the challenges that technological advances in information distribution and communication networks pose to Mission Command will be laid out, including an argument on how the previously mentioned leadership traits will enable an operational commander to overcome these challenges. Finally, two historical leadership examples will be briefly examined before final recommendations are made.

Network-Centric Warfare

The originators of the concept of Network-Centric Warfare, Arthur Cebrowski and John Garstka, describe a process inherent to NCW called self-synchronization.[13] A network-enabled force, they argue, will have access to information that significantly increases situational awareness. When this enhanced situational awareness is combined with a clear commander's intent, reasonable ROE, and true unity of effort, forces will naturally coordinate and self-synchronize in order to accomplish the mission without further direction from higher authority.[14] This self-synchronization enabled by NCW will inevitably lead to a decentralization of control[15] that, in fact, supports the tenets of Mission Command. The paradox, however, is that the same network connectivity that works so well to enhance situational awareness at all levels, also provides commanders the ability to interrupt the self-synchronization process with direction from above and micromanage their forces.[16]

Another way it is argued that NCW supports the decentralization of command is due to the enormous amount of information the network distributes and the extremely fast speed at which the information flows,[17] effectively overloading the commander and preventing him from micromanaging.[18] Instead, he will be forced to rely on Mission Command in order to direct his forces. While this argument does have some merit, especially in extremely large and complex operations, it doesn't necessarily hold true in all cases and doesn't automatically insulate a commander from the dangers of micromanagement. For example, during the first few weeks of OIF, the scale of air operations was too extensive to permit

3

centralized control by rear headquarters. During OEF, however, a more modest scale of air operations did lend itself to centralized control.[19] Furthermore, it is not unreasonable to extrapolate a situation in which a commander chooses to centrally control a small, critical portion of a larger operation, thus diminishing the effects of the information overload and enabling micromanagement. Before a more thorough discussion of the effects of increased connectivity on Mission Command is undertaken, however, it would be helpful to engage in a more detailed discussion of the leadership philosophy of Mission Command.

Mission Command

Mission Command can be defined as the use of mission-type orders to promote decentralized execution of military operations by subordinates who use disciplined initiative and a shared understanding in order to independently carry out the commander's clearly articulated intent.[20] Guiding the execution of Mission Command are the principles of commander's intent, mission orders, shared understanding, mutual trust, disciplined initiative, and prudent risk.[21] By examining each of these principles, a deeper understanding of Mission Command will emerge, and the leadership traits that best equip a commander to effectively execute Mission Command in the Information Age will become more apparent.

Mission Command flows from and is centered on the commander,[22] so it is only natural to begin with commander's intent. Commander's intent should capture the purpose of the mission and the desired end state that the commander hopes to achieve.[23] It should be a clear and concise representation of the commander's own words, and should be delivered in person if at all possible.[24] By delivering his intent in person, subordinates will be able to benefit from verbal and nonverbal cues like voice inflection, tone of voice, physical gestures, and overall body language.[25] This will enable subordinates to put the commander's words in

4

context, obtain immediate clarification if necessary, and contribute to a shared understanding of the commander's vision.[26] From his intent, the commander will then craft mission orders.

A commander's mission orders describe the five W's of the mission – who, what, when, where, and why.[27] From this very basic definition, three important points need to be emphasized. First, the five W's can be broken up into two parts. The first four W's describe the actual task to be carried out, while the last W describes the purpose, or intent, of the mission. Second, the purpose is significantly more important than the task. As the situation develops, the task may need to be modified in order to stay in line with the overarching intent.[28] Third, it is extremely important to notice what is not included in the commander's mission orders - the how. Mission orders should tell subordinates the task they are to accomplish and the reason behind it, but should specifically refrain from telling them how they are to accomplish it. This allows subordinates to exercise their own initiative[29] and promotes the decentralized execution that Mission Command is designed to achieve.[30]

It should be noted, however, that the freedom of action given to subordinates through mission orders requires a shared understanding to ensure that the commander's intent is carried out and that higher objectives are supported.[31] That shared understanding must be created by the commander and can only be accomplished over time. A commander must personally interact with his subordinates and effectively communicate not only his ideas, but also his values and thought processes. He must encourage that same willingness to communicate vertically back up the chain of command and horizontally amongst his subordinates. He must also establish a climate of collaboration that encourages participation in all aspects of planning and operations. By working towards a common goal, the human connections and common experiences created will lead to a shared understanding.[32]

By creating a shared understanding, the commander also lays the foundation for the building of mutual trust. The same processes that work to create shared understanding also, by their nature, significantly contribute to the creation of mutual trust. Mutual trust requires more, however. It requires the demonstration of certain personal qualities by both the commander and his subordinates like integrity, judgment, and professional ability. Most importantly, it is earned through action. Every action, no matter how small, taken by both a leader and his subordinates will either build up or tear down trust to some extent.[33] Finally, trust itself is like a muscle that must be exercised. When a commander trusts his subordinates, it empowers them and motivates them to live up to that trust. When they do live up to it, it makes it easier for the commander to demonstrate that trust again in the future. Furthermore, when a commander supports the decisions and actions of his subordinates, it builds their trust in him and encourages them to show initiative in the future.[34]

A disciplined initiative by subordinates enables decentralized execution, one of the goals of mission command. A commander cannot be in all places at all times. In addition to this fact, more often than not a less experienced, less capable person in the middle of the action will make a better and timelier decision than someone far removed from the situation.[35] For this reason, subordinates are encouraged to exercise initiative when current orders are insufficient to accomplish the mission due to unforeseen factors. The initiative must be disciplined, however, in the sense that it is informed by a shared understanding, is empowered by a mutual trust, and remains within the bounds of the commander's intent. By encouraging his subordinates to take the initiative, it enables the commander to remain focused on the big picture and keep his eye on the overall objective.[36] This form of decentralized execution is not without risks, however.

The "fog of war" is a term used to describe the inherent uncertainty that exists in combat.[37] That uncertainty eventually translates into some form of risk.[38] A prudent risk is one whose potential cost is acceptable relative to the potential impact to mission accomplishment. A commander must be willing to accept prudent risks in order to seize opportunities.[39] One type of uncertainty a commander must deal with occurs whenever he executes Mission Command. The act of empowering a subordinate through mission orders to act based on his intent brings with it the uncertainty of the subordinate's actions and the risk of undesired results.[40] A commander can mitigate that risk through the application of some of the principles previously discussed like clear intent and shared understanding, but will never be able to totally eliminate it. He must therefore make the decision of whether the benefits derived from Mission Command outweigh the risks of decentralized execution.[41]

Leadership Traits

As we conclude our general discussion of Mission Command with the principle of prudent risk, it is only fitting that the first leadership trait we will examine is boldness. Unfortunately, boldness is a term that can mean different things to different people, so a common definition must be agreed upon to facilitate the discussion. The New Oxford American Dictionary defines bold, or boldness, as "showing an ability to take risks; confident and courageous."[42] As if recognizing the fact that there is confusion as to the true meaning of the word, they take the somewhat uncommon step of adding an insert immediately following the definition that compares bold to several other words, including aggressive and audacious. While the words admittedly share similar characteristics, aggressive suggests a menacing or pushy behavior and audacious suggests behavior bordering on recklessness. Bold, on the other hand, has a wider degree of meaning but often suggests a courageous, daring temperament.[43] Recklessness, it should be noted, is defined as "without thinking or caring about the consequences of an action."[44]

For the purpose of this discussion, boldness will be defined as a daring temperament in the face of uncertainty that demonstrates the moral courage and judgment to accept calculated risks in order to seize valuable opportunities. Boldness implies a confidence in decisions, but is mindful of and willing to accept responsibility for the consequences of those decisions. While boldness may often take an active/outward form as when a commander personally leads his troops into battle, it may also manifest itself in a passive form, sometimes called nerve. Nerve enables a leader to show restraint in the face of risk, like when he trusts his subordinates to exercise disciplined initiative in support of his intent.[45]

The other leadership trait that we will examine is interpersonal communication skills. The New Oxford American Dictionary defines interpersonal as "relating to relationships or communication between people,"[46] and communication as "the imparting or exchange of information."[47] Fortunately, these terms do not excite the same controversy as boldness. So with those two definitions in mind, we can define interpersonal communication skills as the ability to exchange information through personal relationships. While this definition appears rather simple and straightforward, it fails to capture the actual complexity of interpersonal communication and the vast amount of research that has attempted to shed light on this critical human interaction.

People start learning how to communicate right from early childhood. It is a fairly automatic process, where good and bad communication habits are developed from their experiences. Unfortunately, the bad habits, which they may be completely unaware of, can severely hamper interpersonal communication. In contrast to how they are developed, reversing bad habits and developing effective interpersonal communication skills is not necessarily automatic, however.[48] Therefore, a commander must make a conscious effort to be aware of how he is communicating both verbally and nonverbally.[49] He must also be aware of the feedback his subordinates are giving by engaging in active listening and by observing their reactions.[50] By understanding how verbal and nonverbal communication is being received by others, a commander can minimize the degree of misunderstanding, and ensure the true meaning and intent of his message are clearly received.[51]

A commander must also be aware that interpersonal communication is shaped and influenced by the environment. Communicating with subordinates during the course of a normal work schedule may facilitate the understanding of a commander's explicit intent, but it will be insufficient to develop a fully shared understanding. That requires an understanding of implicit intent, the foundations of which are most readily gained during events like casual conversations, informal briefings, operational exercises, and unit gatherings.[52] By consciously and actively engaging in effective interpersonal communication during all interactions with his subordinates, a commander will be able to develop a shared understanding and lay the groundwork for establishing mutual trust.

Now that we have a better understanding of the leadership traits of boldness and interpersonal communication skills, we can more fully analyze how these traits help a commander overcome the obstacles to executing Mission Command.

Information Age Challenges

The last quarter century has seen the dawn of the Information Age, which has brought increased connectivity to the military and the world. It is undeniable that increased connectivity has had several positive results, but it has also come with its challenges. The leadership philosophy of Mission Command has not been immune to these challenges.

The first aspect of the Information Age that poses a challenge to effective Mission Command is the global connectivity created by the Internet[53] and the 24-hour news cycle.[54] Not only has the media increased its presence all over the world and embedded itself within nearly all military operations, almost every individual has access to some form of electronic device that can deliver information to the media or directly to the Internet. The speed with which that information travels over the internet and news media means that the effects of even the smallest military engagement can become known to the entire world within minutes and have immediate strategic implications. That fact can, and often does, lead to a risk-averse attitude and a move towards increased centralized control and micromanagement.[55] Furthermore, the desire to avoid such a situation can lead commanders to be intolerant of subordinates' mistakes and perpetuate a "zero defects" mentality that can stifle initiative.[56]

The term "CNN effect" was coined to describe the media's ability to influence strategic policy and military operations.[57] An example of the effect occurred in Mogadishu, Somalia, where gruesome pictures of a dead American soldier were broadcast on television. As a result, American public opinion became firmly opposed to the president's handling of the operation and a decision was made to remove American troops at the earliest opportunity.[58] This effect is not dissimilar to another previously discussed term, Strategic Corporal, that has come to reflect the same situation from a different perspective.[59]

From our earlier examination of Mission Command, we can see three principles that are challenged by the effects of global connectivity. First, the ability to accept prudent risk is replaced by the tendency towards a risk-averse attitude. Second, disciplined initiative is inhibited by a "zero defects" mentality created by the commander's intolerance to mistakes and risk. Third, mutual trust is degraded. The commander displays a lack of trust in his subordinates and the subordinates are unable to trust the commander to back them up when honest mistakes are made in an attempt to carry out the commander's intent.

Looking back at our leadership traits, it is apparent that a bold commander would be better equipped to handle this challenge. First and foremost, he would exhibit a daring temperament that would not shrink from risk when a worthwhile opportunity presented itself. Furthermore, he would have the nerve to empower his subordinates to exercise disciplined initiative even though he knows there would be the possibility of mistakes. Finally, he would take responsibility for his decisions and for the actions of his subordinates, thus strengthening the bond of mutual trust and setting the conditions for effective Mission Command.

The second aspect of the Information Age that poses a challenge to Mission Command is the increased connectivity within the military resulting from the development of a network-enabled force.[60] Leveraging technological advances in communication to enhance battlefield command and control is not a new phenomenon, however. From telegraphs, to radios, and now to satellite communication, commanders have increasingly exploited the ability to command and control their forces from more distant headquarters. This has had the effect of weakening the bond between a commander and his troops, while at the same time enabling a greater centralized control over a larger number of forces.[61]

The dawning of the Information Age has seen a quantum leap in this capability that far surpasses anything previous generations have experienced. Commanders now enjoy unprecedented connectivity and access to information through the Global Command and Control System. They are able to track the location of all friendly and known enemy forces, and observe live video feeds from numerous unmanned systems throughout the operating area.[62] It was thought by some, especially proponents of Network-Centric Warfare, that the increase in situational awareness and connectivity, not only of the commander but between all members of the military, would lead to a decrease in uncertainty, an increase in initiative, and a natural decentralization of operations. Too often, however, commanders have leveraged this capability in order to insert themselves into the lowest tactical levels and micromanage operations.[63] This has given rise to the image of commanders directing operations with an "8,000 mile long screwdriver."[64] It has also resulted in the coining of the term Tactical General, in contrast to the previously mentioned Strategic Corporal.[65]

One telling example of this type of micromanagement involves a four star general who personally directed an airstrike on two insurgent leaders after watching two hours of Predator footage at his headquarters. He controlled every aspect of the tactical operation down to the size of the bomb being dropped.[66] His rationale was that any operation he was responsible for required his personal leadership.[67] Another example occurred during the initial phases of OIF. From his headquarters in Tampa, the CENTCOM commander observed a Blue Force Tracker display that showed both U.S. and Iraqi forces, and noted what he believed to be several U.S. units neither moving nor engaged in hostilities. After reprimanding his ground force commander concerning the stagnation of those units, it was discovered that they were actually engaged in fierce combat with the enemy and that the scale of the blue force tracker map prevented the proper display of the Iraqi forces.[68]

From these two examples, we can see that the motivation to micromanage is not always due to strategic risk aversion, but can also be due to a lack of trust in a subordinate's ability to carry out the commander's intent and the perception that the commander can do the job better himself. Furthermore, the extraordinary amount of information at the commander's fingertips can lead to a false sense of omniscience that often results in a gross misinterpretation of battlefield realities. Finally, the sophistication of the network gives the commander extraordinary capability to micromanage operations if he desires.

Leveraging our previous examination of Mission Command again, we can see three principles that are challenged by the effects of a network-enabled force. The first is a shared understanding. Even though technological advances have provided the commander with infinitely more information and control, it has also led to increased distance between a commander and his troops, both in physical and relational terms. A shared understanding can only truly be established by personal interaction in which a commander shares his ideas, values, and thought processes, and also gains insight into his subordinates' capabilities, motivation, and understanding. A shared understanding is also the foundation for, and a large component, of mutual trust. Without truly knowing his subordinates, it is difficult for a commander to extend the trust necessary for Mission Command to flourish. Finally, when subordinates know that their commander can, and will, interfere in their operations at any time, it stifles the initiative of the subordinates, another prerequisite for Mission Command.

A commander that develops and prioritizes the use of interpersonal communication skills will be better able to bridge the relationship gap created by technology. He will seek every opportunity to personally interact with his subordinates and maximize the use of those skills to create a relationship that fosters the understanding of his explicit and implicit intent. He will also use those skills to know his people better, which will enhance his confidence in them and create an understanding that goes both ways. Realizing that he will not be able to always interact with them in person, he will modify and leverage his communication network to provide additional opportunities to build relationships instead of just focusing on the network's ability to transfer information and execute control. Furthermore, the shared understanding that he creates will be instrumental to the building of mutual trust and decrease the motivation to micromanage. Finally, when subordinates recognize that their commander will not take advantage of his ability to interfere in their operations, it will motivate them to execute the disciplined initiative that is so critical to Mission Command.

Historical Examples

Now that we have seen how the traits of boldness and interpersonal communication skills can better equip a leader to execute Mission Command, it would be helpful to briefly examine historical examples that show the benefits of these traits, as well as the dangers that exist when they are lacking. We will look at Admiral Horatio Lord Nelson during the Battle of Trafalgar, and at General Wesley Clark during Operation ALLIED FORCE (OAF).

At the Battle of Trafalgar in 1805, Nelson commanded only 27 British ships against 33 French and Spanish ships[69] that had more guns and better armor.[70] His ships were more maneuverable, however, and had superior captains, sailors and gun crews.[71] Realizing that his lighter, out-gunned ships would be vulnerable using standard line of battle tactics,[72] Nelson devised a bold but risky plan to divide his forces into two groups[73] and sail perpendicular to the enemy line of ships. By breaking through their lines, he would inflict severe damage and transform the battle into a series of smaller, dynamic engagements that would favor his maneuverable ships and the skill of his superior captains and sailors.[74]

In preparation for battle, he held a series of dinners with both senior and junior subordinates in order to build rapport,[75] and then dedicated significant time and effort to explain his tactical concepts.[76] He realized that his plan would rely on the decision making of his captains,[77] and so crafted simple intent that included "no Captain can do very wrong if he places his Ship alongside that of an Enemy."[78] He boldly placed his trust in his captains, and due to his clear intent, his personal qualities as a leader, and the shared understanding he had created, his subordinates placed their trust in him.[79] Even though Nelson died less than an hour into the battle,[80] that mutual trust was rewarded with a resounding victory[81] in which Nelson's captains exercised decisive initiative in support of his intent.

While Nelson certainly displayed boldness in his actions and his nerve, and expertly used interpersonal communication skills in order to create a shared understanding that led to mutual trust, evidence of these traits appears to be lacking in General Clark's handling of Operation ALLIED FORCE in 1999. The operation saw nearly every instance of collateral damage exaggerated in the media[82] and was also the first time video teleconferencing was used on such a large scale,[83] both of which magnified the impact of these deficiencies.

OAF consisted of a 78-day NATO air campaign against Yugoslavia in an effort to stop human rights violations in Kosovo.[84] From the very beginning, it was influenced by a fragile NATO alliance[85] and unprecedented political pressure to avoid loss of civilian lives and damage to civilian infrastructure,[86] which negatively impacted the operational and tactical levels of war.[87] While his position as SACEUR forced General Clark to deal with the political realities, he also elected to personally direct the air campaign from Brussels.[88] In addition to selecting targets, he even adjusted individual impact points[89] and chose the types of weapons used.[90] This lack of boldness, or nerve, to rely on subordinates resulted in an aggressive micromanagement that severely impacted their ability to contribute to the effort.[91]

One of the avenues of this micromanagement was the VTC, occurring as many as three to four times a day.[92] During this time, detailed examination of the target list would occur,[93] and it would often be the only time General Clark was able to speak to his subordinate commanders. Instead of using the opportunity to leverage interpersonal communication skills to deliver a clear intent, build relationships, and develop a shared understanding, the technology was used to micromanage operations, which often resulted in misunderstanding down the chain of command and excessive, unproductive staff work.[94]

The Way Forward

From our examination of the principles of Mission Command and the challenges that Information Age technologies pose to its effective implementation, we have seen how the leadership traits of boldness and interpersonal communication skills best enable an operational commander to overcome those challenges and stay true to the principles of Mission Command. When those traits are lacking, leaders will be more likely to fall into the trap of micromanagement, which is in direct opposition to the leadership philosophy of Mission Command and the Chairman of the Joint Chiefs of Staff's vision for Joint Force 2020. Therefore, measures must be taken to instill these qualities in our future leaders.

The senior leaders of all U.S. military services must emphasize the importance of the leadership traits of boldness and interpersonal communication skills. These traits must be developed from the beginning of an officer's career through appropriate training and mentorship, and the possession of these qualities should be weighed heavily in determining advancement. Furthermore, senior leaders must instill a culture of tolerance for honest mistakes that arise from bold action and actively oppose a "zero defects" mentality. They must also continue to stress that our military's greatest strength is not our technology, but is and always will be our people, and therefore, all leaders must use good interpersonal communication skills to develop relationships that will harness that strength.

Operational training exercises must be tailored to provide opportunities for commanders and their subordinates to develop the quality of boldness. Scenarios should be constructed in a way in which it is impossible to mitigate all risk and a decision whether to accept that risk must be made. The identification, evaluation and taking of prudent risk in order to accomplish the objective should be prioritized, with positive reinforcement provided for bold decisions and actions even when unfavorable results occur.

While personal interaction with subordinates should be the primary means of developing meaningful relationships and a shared understanding, operational commanders must also leverage their communication networks. Instead of relying on the networks simply to facilitate the transfer of information and the exercise of control, commanders should focus on the network's ability to supplement these personal interactions. While admittedly not the most ideal environment, there are many ways in which interpersonal communication skills do translate across electronic media, especially when sound is combined with video, as in a video teleconference. Many verbal and nonverbal cues can still be observed that give insight into a commander's true meaning and also reveal a subordinate's level of understanding. When these events are used to discuss things like ideas, values, and thought processes instead of mundane administrative and operational issues, a commander will be able to exploit an additional avenue to develop meaningful relationships and a shared understanding.

The execution of Mission Command is an ideal often aspired to but not easily achieved. By developing the leadership traits of boldness and interpersonal communication skills, operational commanders will be better able to harness this leadership philosophy's full potential and usher in the realization of Joint Force 2020.

NOTES

[1] General Martin E. Dempsey, "Mission Command White Paper," (April 2012): 3. Accessed 17 May 2013. http://www.jcs.mil/content/files/2012-04/042312114128_CJCS_Mission_Command_White_Paper_2012_a.pdf.

[2] Ibid.

[3] Edgar Vincent, "Nelson and Mission Command," *History Today* 53, no. 6 (June 2003): 18.

[4] Chairman, U.S. Joint Chiefs of Staff, *Joint Operations* (Joint Publication 3-0, Washington DC: CJCS, 11 August 2011), II-2.

[5] U.S. Army, *Mission Command* (Army Doctrine Publication (ADP) 6-0, Washington DC: Department of the Army, 17 May 2012), 1.

[6] U.S. Marine Corps, *Marine Corps Operations* (Marine Corps Doctrine Publication (MCDP) 1-0, Washington DC: Department of the Navy, Headquarters United States Marine Corps, 9 August 2011), 1-3.

[7] Art Corbett, "Mission Command," 1. Accessed 17 May 2013. https://www.nwdc.navy.mil/ncoi/mis/Briefs/Corbett%20-%20Mission%20Command%20document.pdf

[8] Dempsey, "Mission Command White Paper," 3.

[9] John Manchester, "The Strategic Corporal vs. The Strategic Cameraman," *Small Wars Journal Blog Post*, 8 May 2007, accessed 17 May 2013, http://smallwarsjournal.com/blog/the-strategic-corporal-vs-the-strategic-cameraman

[10] P.W. Singer, "Tactical Generals: Leaders, Technology, and the Perils of Battlefield Management*," *Air & Space Power Journal* 23, no. 2 (Summer 2009): 80.

[11] Dempsey, "Mission Command White Paper," 5-6.

[12] Ibid, 6.

[13] Arthur K. Cebrowski and John J. Garstka, "Network-Centric Warfare: Its Origin and Future," *United States Naval Institute. Proceedings* 124, no. 1 (January 1998): 28-35.

[14] Ibid.

[15] David S. Alberts, "NWC Further Defined," *Aviation Week & Space Technology* 164, no.6 (February 2006): 6.

[16] Jennifer Free, "Network-Centric Leadership: Why Trust Is Essential," *United States Naval Institute. Proceedings* 131, no. 6 (June 2005): 60.

[17] Jim Mele, "M2M," *Fleet Owner* 100, no. 6 (June 2005): 81.

[18] Major J. S. Meiter, "Network Enabled Capability: A Theory in Need of a Doctrine," *Defence Studies* 6, no. 2 (June 2006): 198.

[19] Benjamin S. Lambeth, "The Downside of Network-Centric Warfare," *Aviation Week & Space Technology* 164, no. 1 (January 2006): 86.

[20] Chairman, U.S. Joint Chiefs of Staff. *Joint Operations*, II-2.

[21] U.S. Army, *Mission Command* (Army Doctrine Reference Publication (ADRP) 6-0, Washington DC: Department of the Army, 17 May 2012), 2-1.

[22] Dempsey, "Mission Command White Paper," 4.

[23] U.S. Army, *Mission Command (ADP), 3.*

[24] U.S. Army, *Mission Command (ADRP), 2-3.*

[25] U.S. Marine Corps, *Warfighting* (Marine Corps Doctrine Publication (MCDP) 1, Washington DC: Department of the Navy, Headquarters United States Marine Corps, 20 June 1997), 79.

[26] U.S. Army, *Mission Command (ADRP), 2-3.*

[27] Ibid, 2-5.

[28] U.S. Marine Corps, *Warfighting, 89.*

[29] U.S. Army, *Mission Command (ADRP), 2-4.*

[30] Art Corbett, "Mission Command," 10.

[31] U.S. Marine Corps, *Warfighting, 88.*

[32] U.S. Army, *Mission Command (ADRP), 2-2.*

[33] Ibid, 2-1.

[34] Ibid, 2-2.

[35] Art Corbett, "Mission Command," 12.

[36] U.S. Army, *Mission Command (ADRP)*, 2-4.

[37] U.S. Marine Corps, *Warfighting, 7.*

[38] Ibid, 8.

[39] U.S. Army, *Mission Command (ADP), 5.*

[40] U.S. Army, *Mission Command (ADRP)*, 2-9.

[41] Ibid, 2-16.

[42] Erin McKean, *The New Oxford American Dictionary*, 2nd ed. (New York, NY: Oxford University Press, 2005), 189.

[43] Ibid.

[44] Ibid, 1414.

[45] Art Corbett, "Mission Command," 20.

[46] Erin McKean, *The New Oxford American Dictionary, 881.*

[47] Ibid, 344.

[48] William D. Brooks and Philip Emmert, *Interpersonal Communication* (Dubuque, IA: Wm. C. Brown Company Publishers, 1976), 4.

[49] Ibid, 31.

[50] Ibid, 148.

[51] John J. Makay and Beverly A. Gaw, *Personal and Interpersonal Communication.* (Columbus, OH: Charles E. Merrill Publishing Company, 1975), 103.

[52] Bjorn J. E. Johansson and Per-Arne Persson, "Reduced Uncertainty Through Human Communication in Complex Environments," *Cognition, Technology & Work* (2009): 208.

[53] John Manchester, "The Strategic Corporal vs. The Strategic Cameraman,"

[54] General (Retired) Gary Luck, and The JS J7 Deployable Training Division. *Mission Command and Cross-Domain Synergy.* Insights and Best Practices Focus Paper, March 2013, 3. Accessed 17 May 2013. http://www.dtic.mil/doctrine/fp/mission_command_fp.pdf

[55] Ibid.

[56] Linda D. Kozaryn, "Perry Says Military Needs Bold, Daring Leaders." *American Forces Press Service,* 6 August 1996. Accessed 17 May 2013. http://www.defense.gov/News/NewsArticle.aspx?ID=40748

[57] Steven Livingston, *Clarifying the CNN Effect: An Examination of the Media Effects According to Type of Military Intervention*, Research Paper R-18 (Boston, MA: President and Fellows of Harvard College, 1997), 1.

[58] Ibid, 4.

[59] John Manchester, "The Strategic Corporal vs. The Strategic Cameraman,"

[60] Dempsey, "Mission Command White Paper," 3.

[61] P.W. Singer, "Tactical Generals: Leaders, Technology, and the Perils of Battlefield Management*," 79.

[62] Ibid.

[63] Ibid, 80.

[64] Benjamin S. Lambeth, "The Downside of Network-Centric Warfare," 86.

[65] P.W. Singer, "Tactical Generals: Leaders, Technology, and the Perils of Battlefield Management*," 80.

[66] Ibid, 78.

[67] Ibid, 80.

[68] Ibid, 81.

[69] Ruddock Mackay and Michael Duffy, *Hawk, Nelson, and British Naval Leadership, 1747-1805*, (UK: The Boydell Press, 2009), 211.

[70] David S. Alberts and Richard E. Hayes, *Power to the Edge: Command...Control...in the Information Age*, (Washington, D.C.: Command and Control Research Program, 2005), 28. Accessed 17 May 2013. http://www.dodccrp.org/files/Alberts_Power.pdf

[71] Ibid, 29.

[72] Ibid, 28.

[73] Edgar Vincent, "Nelson and Mission Command,"

[74] David S. Alberts and Richard E. Hayes, *Power to the Edge: Command...Control...in the Information Age*, 29.

[75] Ruddock Mackay and Michael Duffy, *Hawk, Nelson, and British Naval Leadership, 1747-1805*, 208-209.

[76] Ibid, 210.

[77] Ibid, 211.

[78] Ibid, 211.

[79] Edgar Vincent, "Nelson and Mission Command," 19.

[80] Ibid.

[81] David S. Alberts and Richard E. Hayes, *Power to the Edge: Command...Control...in the Information Age*, 31.

[82] Benjamin S. Lambeth, *NATO's Air War for Kosovo: A Strategic and Operational Assessment*, (2001; repr., Rand, 2001), 139. http://web.ebscohost.com/ehost/ebookviewer/ebook/nlebk_72762_AN?sid=1a00f727-7db6-458c-9628-38e12860dbd4@sessionmgr114&vid=1&format=EB

[83] Ibid, 216.

[84] Ibid, xiii.

[85] Don D. Chipman, "General Short and the Politics of Kosovo's Air War," *Air Power History* 49, no. 2 (Summer 2002): 33.

[86] Benjamin S. Lambeth, *NATO's Air War for Kosovo: A Strategic and Operational Assessment*, xvii.

[87] General Wesley K. Clark, *Waging Modern War* (New York: PublicAffairs, 2002), 10.

[88] Benjamin S. Lambeth, *NATO's Air War for Kosovo: A Strategic and Operational Assessment*, 193.

[89] Ibid, 191.

[90] Ibid, 192.

[91] Ibid, 190.

[92] Ibid, 217.

[93] Ibid, 191.

[94] Ibid, 217.

BIBLIOGRAPHY

Alberts, David S. "NWC Further Defined," *Aviation Week & Space Technology* 164, no.6 (February 2006): 6.

Alberts, David S., and Richard E. Hayes. *Power to the Edge: Command...Control...in the Information Age*. Washington, D.C.: Command and Control Research Program, 2005. Accessed 17 May 2013. http://www.dodccrp.org/files/Alberts_Power.pdf

Betz, David. "Clausewitz and Connectivity," *Infinity Journal* 3, no. 1 (Winter 2012): 4-9.

Brooks, William D., and Philip Emmert. *Interpersonal Communication*. Dubuque, IA: Wm. C. Brown Company Publishers, 1976.

Cebrowski, Arthur K., and John J. Garstka, "Network-Centric Warfare: Its Origin and Future," *United States Naval Institute. Proceedings* 124, no. 1 (January 1998): 28-35.

Chairman, U.S. Joint Chiefs of Staff. *Joint Operations,* Joint Publication 3-0, Washington DC: CJCS, 11 August 2011.

Chipman, Don D. "General Short and the Politics of Kosovo's Air War," *Air Power History* 49, no. 2 (Summer 2002): 31-39.

Clark, General Wesley K. *Waging Modern War*. New York: Public Affairs, 2002.

Corbett, Art. "Mission Command." Accessed 17 May 2013. https://www.nwdc.navy.mil/ncoi/mis/Briefs/Corbett%20-%20Mission%20Command%20document.pdf

Dempsey, General Martin E. "Mission Command White Paper." (April 2012): 1-8. Accessed 17 May 2013. http://www.jcs.mil/content/files/2012-04/042312114128_CJCS_Mission_Command_White_Paper_2012_a.pdf.

Free, Jennifer. "Network-Centric Leadership: Why Trust Is Essential," *United States Naval Institute. Proceedings* 131, no. 6 (June 2005): 58-60.

Johansson, Bjorn J. E., and Per-Arne Persson, "Reduced Uncertainty Through Human Communication in Complex Environments," *Cognition, Technology & Work* (2009): (205-214).

Kozaryn, Linda D. "Perry Says Military Needs Bold, Daring Leaders." *American Forces Press Service,* 6 August 1996. Accessed 17 May 2013. http://www.defense.gov/News/NewsArticle.aspx?ID=40748

Lambeth, Benjamin S. "The Downside of Network-Centric Warfare," *Aviation Week &*

Space Technology 164, no. 1 (January 2006): 86.

_____. 2001. *NATO's Air War for Kosovo: A Strategic and Operational Assessment.* Reprint, Rand, 2001. http://web.ebscohost.com/ehost/ebookviewer/ebook/nlebk_72762_AN?sid=1a00f727 -7db6-458c-9628-38e12860dbd4@sessionmgr114&vid=1&format=EB

Livingston, Steven. *Clarifying the CNN Effect: An Examination of the Media Effects According to Type of Military Intervention.* Research Paper R-18. Boston, MA: President and Fellows of Harvard College, 1997.

Luck, General (Retired) Gary, and The JS J7 Deployable Training Division. *Mission Command and Cross-Domain Synergy.* Insights and Best Practices Focus Paper, March 2013. Accessed 17 May 2013. http://www.dtic.mil/doctrine/fp/mission_command_fp.pdf

Mackay, Ruddock and Michael Duffy. *Hawke, Nelson, and British Naval Leadership, 1747-1805.* UK: The Boydell Press, 2009.

Manchester, John. "The Strategic Corporal vs. The Strategic Cameraman," *Small Wars Journal Blog Post*, 8 May 2007. Accessed 17 May 2013, http://smallwarsjournal.com/blog/the-strategic-corporal-vs-the-strategic-cameraman

McKean, Erin. *The New Oxford American Dictionary.* 2nd ed. New York, NY: Oxford University Press, 2005.

Meiter, Major J. S. "Network Enabled Capability: A Theory in Need of a Doctrine," *Defence Studies* 6, no. 2 (June 2006): 189-214.

Mele, Jim. "M2M," *Fleet Owner* 100, no. 6 (June 2005): 81-82, 84.

Potts, David. *The Big Issue: Command and Combat in the Information Age.* Washington, D.C.: Command and Control Research Program, 2002. Accessed 17 May 2013. http://www.dodccrp.org/files/Potts_Big_Issue.pdf

Ropski, Janusz. "Interpersonal Competence in Commanding," *Science & Military Journal* 3 no.1 (January 2008): 34-38.

Schmitt, Capt John F. "Observations on Decisionmaking in Battle," *Marine Corps Gazette* 72 no. 3 (March 1988): 18-20.

Singer, P.W. "Tactical Generals: Leaders, Technology, and the Perils of Battlefield Management*." *Air & Space Power Journal* 23 no. 2 (Summer 2009): 78-87, 127.

U.S. Marine Corps. *Marine Corps Operations.* Marine Corps Doctrine Publication (MCDP)

1-0, Washington DC: Department of the Navy, Headquarters United States Marine Corps, 9 August 2011.

_____. *Warfighting.* Marine Corps Doctrine Publication (MCDP) 1, Washington DC: Department of the Navy, Headquarters United States Marine Corps, 20 June 1997.

U.S. Army. *Mission Command.* Army Doctrine Publication (ADP) 6-0, Washington DC: Department of the Army, 17 May 2012.

_____. *Mission Command.* Army Doctrine Reference Publication (ADRP) 6-0, Washington DC: Department of the Army, 17 May 2012.

Vincent, Edgar. "Nelson and Mission Command," *History Today* 53, no. 6 (June 2003): 18-19.